CU00727241

First Published In 2021 By Travis Whitehead

© Travis Whitehead

The information provided herein is stated to be truthful and consistent, in that any liability, in terms of inattention or otherwise, by any usage or abuse of any policies, processes, or directions contained within is the solitary and utter responsibility of the recipient reader. Under no circumstances will any legal responsibility or blame be held against the publisher for any reparation, damages, or monetary loss due to the information herein, either directly or indirectly. Respective authors own all copyrights not held by the publisher.

The information herein is offered for informational purposes solely and is universal as so. The presentation of the information is without contract or any type of guarantee assurance. The trademarks that are used are without any consent, and the publication of the trademark is without permission or backing by the trademark owner. All trademarks and brands within this book are for clarifying purposes only and are the owned by the owners themselves, not affiliated with this document.

CONTENTS

INTRODUCTION

There's nothing like having a perfectly grilled steak in front of you at the dinner table, but you don't have to go outside to cook it! There are lots of fantastic electric grill cooking tips that can turn your kitchen into the perfect indoor grill. The best part is that you don't have to buy expensive gadgets to do it!

Here are thirteen electric home grilling tips you can put to use right now. These easy tips simplify your meal preparation, and they will improve your cooking skills!

Top 13 Indoor Grilling Tips for Newbies

1. Pan-Sear Your Meats Before Grilling In The Oven

One of the first things you should realize when cooking meats is how to bring out the natural flavors. The easiest way to imitate the robust flavor of outdoor grilling is by searing your meats in a pan before you place them in an oven grill.

Put a little of your favorite oil in a cast iron pan along with some seasonings. Let the pan heat, and fry the outer-layer until it's lightly charred. You'll have much more flavor than from traditional oven grilling.

2. Don't Add Salt Until Serving

Salting foods before cooking can seriously affect the texture of your dish. It can remove too much moisture from vegetables, and it can toughen the texture of red meats. You should avoid adding any salts to your meal until it's completely done.

This electric grill tip applies to seasonings as well. You're going to lose a lot of liquid content from grilling. The last thing you want is a dry chicken breast with strong flavors.

3. Add Butter And Olive Oil For Flavor

It might seem a little pointless to add oils on a steak you're cooking on an electric tabletop grill. The main point of using one is to remove all of those unhealthy fats, but certain oils really improve a dish. It's not going to seriously impact the healthy aspects of indoor grilling to add a splash of oil.

Most of the oils you add are going to be cooked away. It's really about adding complexity to your pallet. Your guests will definitely pick up on the subtle hints of olive oil, but they won't have to worry much about counting calories.

4. Cast Iron Grilling

If you're looking for a more visual appeal, then you should try using a cast iron grill pan. You can pick one up at virtually any kitchen supply store. These cast iron skillets are typically flat with lots of raised lines to create that iconic look.

Presentation is half of the process. You'll want your foods to taste great, and you'll want them to look pretty on the plate. This is one of those indoor grill tips that could get your next t-bone its own photo-shoot from the family.

5. Fat Draining Electric Tabletop Grills

This is probably the most underrated type of appliance in your kitchen. It's a lot better than most people realize. Your meats get cooked super-fast because it's pretty much pressing two hot plates together on both sides. The downside is that it can be frustrating to clean afterward.

One of the more helpful electric grill tips is to use heatproof parchment paper to cover your meat in before you cook it. This keeps your electric tabletop grill perfectly clean without having to scrub away burnt on grease.

6. Smoked Seasonings

All of the indoor grill tips in the world can't put that smokey flavor you get from charcoal, but smoked seasonings certainly can! Keep it simple. Just add a little smoked paprika to your regular seasonings for a nice kick.

A good quality chipotle marinade can really take your dish to the next level. Try to avoid adding liquid smoke to meats because it can overpower the flavor of beef.

7. Preheat The Grill

You should always preheat the electric grill you're using to a fairly hot temperature. Never put cold meat on a cold cooking surface. This is one of the professional electric grill cooking tips that a lot of people don't know about.

A faster cook time means that your foods will retain their moisture levels better than slowly heating up the cooking surface with the meat. Improper heating of the pan can also cause the meat to cook unevenly. Make sure your electric grill really sizzles when you place uncooked food on it.

8. Grilled And Steamed Veggies

Don't forget that your indoor grill is great for cooking a variety of veggies. Try wrapping your broccoli in a parchment paper the next time you grill. You can get the same tenderness that you would from steaming, but with the added bonus of a little charred flavor.

9. Try A Food Torch

You'll definitely leave an impression on your dinner guests if you pull out a food torch to top off their succulent meal. It's a really showy way to imitate the flame-broiled tastes of a propane grill. Just be sure to stay safe while you set the food on fire.

Always make sure you fully cook any meats you put on the grill. The ThermoPro Food Thermometer company makes a whole bunch of different gadgets that'll have you feeling like a culinary master. It's always better to be safe than sorry.

BREAKFAST RECIPES

Bacon

Servings: 3
Cooking Time: 10 Minutes

Ingredients:
- 2 tablespoons water
- 6 slices bacon

Directions:
1. Pour water to the bottom of the Ninja Foodi Grill pot.
2. Place the grill rack inside.
3. Put the bacon slices on the grill rack.
4. Select air fry function.
5. Cook at 350 degrees F for 5 minutes per side or until golden and crispy.

Avocado Toast

Servings: 1
Cooking Time: 3 Minutes

Ingredients:
- 1 avocado, mashed
- 1 clove garlic, minced
- 1 teaspoon lemon juice
- Salt to taste
- 2 slices bread
- ¼ cup tomato, chopped

Directions:
1. Mix the avocado, garlic, lemon juice, salt and pepper.
2. Spread mixture on top of bread slices.
3. Sprinkle tomato on top.
4. Add to the grill grate.
5. Press grill setting.
6. Grill at 350 degrees F for 2 to 3 minutes.

Chocolate Granola

Servings: 20
Cooking Time: 2 Hours

Ingredients:

- 5 cups unsweetened coconut, shredded 1 cup almonds, chopped
- 1/3 cups sunflower seeds
- 1/3 cups pumpkin seeds
- ¼ cup cacao nibs
- 2½ ounces coconut oil, melted
- 3 tablespoons Erythritol
- 4 tablespoons cocoa powder unsweetened 1 tablespoon lemon zest, grated finely

Directions:

1. In the pot of Ninja Foodi, add all ingredients and mix well.
2. Close the Ninja Foodi with a crisping lid and select "Slow Cooker".
3. Set on "High" for 2 hours.
4. Press "Start/Stop" to begin cooking.
5. Stir the mixture after every 15 minutes.
6. Move the granola onto an enormous heating sheet and set aside to cool completely before serving.

Nuts & Seeds Granola

Servings: 12
Cooking Time: 2 Hours

Ingredients:

- 1/3 cup unsalted butter
- 1 teaspoon liquid stevia
- 1 teaspoon organic vanilla extract
- 1½ cups pumpkin seeds
- 1½ cups sunflower seeds
- ½ cup raw pecans, chopped roughly
- ½ cup raw hazelnuts, chopped roughly
- ½ cup raw walnuts, chopped roughly
- ½ cup raw almonds, chopped roughly
- 1 teaspoon ground cinnamon

Directions:

1. Select the "Sauté/Sear" setting of Ninja Foodi and place the butter into the pot.
2. Press "Start/Stop" to begin cooking and heat for about 2-3 minutes.
3. Include the fluid stevia and vanilla concentrate and mix to combine.
4. Immediately, press "Start/Stop" to stop cooking
5. Now, add the remaining ingredients and stir to combine.
6. Close the Ninja Foodi with a crisping lid and select "Slow Cooker".
7. Set on "Low" for 2 hours, stirring after every 30 minutes.
8. Press "Start/Stop" to begin cooking.
9. Move the granola onto an enormous heating sheet and set aside to cool completely before serving.

Zucchini & Coconut Bread

Servings: 10
Cooking Time: 3 Hours

Ingredients:

- 2½ cups zucchini, shredded
- ½ teaspoon salt
- 1 1/3 cups almond flour
- 2/3 cup coconut, shredded
- 2 teaspoons ground cinnamon
- ½ teaspoon ground ginger
- ¼ teaspoon ground nutmeg
- 3 large organic eggs
- ¼ cup butter, melted
- ¼ cup water
- ½ teaspoon organic vanilla extract
- ½ cup walnuts, chopped

Directions:

1. Arrange a large sieve in a sink.
2. Place the zucchini in a sieve and sprinkle with salt. Set aside to drain for about 1 hour.
3. With your hands, squeeze out the moisture from zucchini.
4. In a large bowl, add the almond flour, coconut, Erythritol, protein powder, baking powder, and spices and mix well.
5. Add the zucchini, eggs, coconut oil, water, and vanilla extract and mix until well combined.
6. Fold in the walnuts.
7. At the bottom of a greased Ninja Foodie, place the mixture.
8. Close the Ninja Foodi with a crisping lid and select "Slow Cooker".
9. Set on "Low" for 2½-3 hours.
10. Press "Start/Stop" to begin cooking.
11. Keep the bread inside for about 5-10 minutes.
12. Carefully, remove the bread from the pot and place onto a wire rack to cool completely before slicing.
13. Cut the bread into desired-sized slices and serve.

Roasted Garlic Potatoes

Servings: 4

Cooking Time: 20 Minutes

Ingredients:

- 2 lb. baby potatoes, sliced into wedges
- 2 tablespoons olive oil
- 2 teaspoons garlic salt

Directions:

1. Toss the potatoes in olive oil and garlic salt. Add the potatoes to the Ninja Foodi basket. Seal the crisping lid. Set it to air crisp. Cook at 390 degrees F for 20 minutes.

Cheesy Broccoli Quiche

Servings: 8
Cooking Time: 40 Minutes

Ingredients:

- 1 cup water
- 2 cups broccoli florets
- 1 carrot, chopped
- 1 cup cheddar cheese, grated
- ¼ cup Feta cheese, crumbled
- ¼ cup milk
- 2 eggs
- 1 teaspoon parsley
- 1 teaspoon thyme
- Salt and pepper to taste

Directions:

1. Pour the water inside the Ninja Foodi. Place the basket inside.
2. Put the carrots and broccoli on the basket. Cover the pot.
3. Set it to pressure. Cook at high pressure for 2 minutes.
4. Release the pressure quickly. Crack the eggs into a bowl and beat.
5. Season with the salt, pepper, parsley, and thyme. Put the vegetables on a small baking pan. Layer with the cheese and pour in the beaten eggs. Place on the basket.
6. Choose the Air Crisp function. Seal the crisping lid. Cook at 350°F for 20 minutes.
7. serving Suggestions:
8. Garnish with chopped parsley or chives.

Sausage Casserole

Servings: 4
Cooking Time: 20 Minutes

Ingredients:

- 1 lb. hash browns
- 2 red bell peppers, chopped
- 1 white onion, chopped
- 4 eggs, beaten
- 1 lb. ground breakfast sausage, cooked
- Salt and pepper to taste

Directions:

1. Line the air fryer basket with foil.
2. Add hash browns at the bottom part.
3. Spread sausage, onion and bell peppers on top.
4. Air fry at 355 degrees F for 10 minutes.
5. Pour eggs on top and cook for another 10 minutes.
6. Season with salt and pepper.

Bacon & Scrambled Eggs

Servings: 4
Cooking Time: 25 Minutes

Ingredients:

- 4 strips bacon
- 2 eggs
- 1 tablespoon milk
- Salt and pepper to taste

Directions:

1. Place the bacon inside the Ninja Foodi. Set it to Air Crisp.
2. Cover the crisping lid. Cook at 390°F for 3 minutes.
3. Flip the bacon and cook for another 2 minutes. Remove the bacon and set aside.
4. Whisk the eggs and milk in a bowl. Season with the salt and pepper.
5. Set the Ninja Foodi to Sauté. Add the eggs and cook until firm.
6. serving Suggestions:
7. Serve with toasted bread.

Healthy Potato Pancakes

Servings: 4
Cooking Time: 24 Minutes

Ingredients:

- Salt and pepper to taste
- 3 tablespoons flour
- ¼ teaspoon salt
- ½ teaspoon garlic powder
- 2 tablespoons unsalted butter
- ¼ cup milk
- 1 egg, beaten
- 1 medium onion, chopped
- 4 medium potatoes, peeled and cleaned

Directions:

1. Take your potatoes and peel them. Shred the potatoes and soak the shredded potatoes under cold water.
2. Drain your potatoes in a colander.
3. In a separate bowl, add milk, eggs, butter, garlic powder, pepper, and salt. Add flour and mix the whole mixture well.
4. Add shredded potatoes.
5. Preheat your Ninja Foodi to Air Crisp mode with a temperature of 390°F, setting the timer to 24 minutes.
6. Once you hear the beep, add ¼ cup of potato pancake batter to the cooking basket.
7. Cook for 12 minutes until you have a nice golden texture.
8. Repeat with remaining batter.
9. Serve once done, enjoy!

French Toast(2)

Servings: 4

Cooking Time: 35 Minutes

Ingredients:

- 2 eggs, beaten
- ¼ cup milk
- ¼ cup brown sugar
- 1 tablespoon honey
- 1 teaspoon cinnamon
- ¼ teaspoon nutmeg
- 4 slices wholemeal bread, sliced into strips

Directions:

1. In a bowl, combine all the ingredients except the bread. Mix well.
2. Dip each strip in the mixture. Place the bread strips in the Ninja Foodi basket.
3. Place basket inside the pot. Cover with the crisping lid. Set it to Air Crisp.
4. Cook at 320°F for 10 minutes.
5. serving Suggestions:
6. Dust with confectioners' sugar.

Low-carb Breakfast Casserole

Servings: 8
Cooking Time: 15min

Ingredients:

- 1 - LB Ground Sausage
- ¼ Cup Diced White Onion
- 1 - Diced Green Bell Pepper
- 8 - Whole Eggs, Beaten
- ½ Cup Shredded Colby Jack Cheese
- 1 - Tsp Fennel Seed
- ½ Tsp Garlic Salt

Directions:

1. On the off threat that you are utilizing the Ninja Foodi, utilize the sauté potential to brown the frankfurter inside the pot of the foodi. In the occasion that you are utilizing a Ninja Foodi, you could make use of a skillet to do that.
2. Include the onion and pepper and prepare dinner along with the ground wiener until the vegetables are sensitive and the hotdog is cooked.
3. Utilizing the 8.75-inch container or the Air Fryer skillet, splash it with a non-stick cooking bathe.
4. Spot the floor wiener mixture on the base of the skillet.
5. Top uniformly with cheddar.
6. Pour the crushed eggs uniformly over the cheddar and frankfurter.
7. Include fennel seed and garlic salt uniformly over the eggs.
8. Spot the rack within the low state of affairs within the Ninja Foodi, and in a while region the box on the pinnacle.
9. Set to Air Crisp for 15MIN at 390 levels.
10. In the occasion which you are using an air fryer, place the dish legitimately into the bin of the air fryer and cook for 15MIN at 390 tiers.
11. Cautiously expel and serve.

Sausage & Bacon Omelet

Servings: 2

Cooking Time: 10 Minutes

Ingredients:

- 4 eggs
- Ground black pepper, as required
- 1 bacon slice, chopped
- 2 sausages, chopped
- 1 onion, chopped
- 1 teaspoon fresh parsley, minced

Directions:

1. In a bowl, crack the eggs and black pepper and beat well.
2. Add the remaining ingredients and gently stir to combine.
3. Place the mixture into a baking pan.
4. Arrange the drip pan at the bottom of the Instant Ninja Foodi Plus Air Fryer Oven cooking chamber.
5. Select "Air Dry" and then adjust the temperature to 320 degrees F.
6. Set the timer for 10 minutes and press the "Start."
7. When the display shows "Add Food," place the baking pan over the drip pan.
8. When the display shows "Turn Food," do nothing.
9. When cooking time is complete, remove the pan from the Ninja Foodi and serve warm.

Breakfast Potatoes

Servings: 4
Cooking Time: 55 Minutes

Ingredients:

- 4 potatoes
- 2 cups cheddar cheese, shredded
- 8 slices bacon, cooked crispy and chopped
- 1 1/4 cups sour cream
- 4 teaspoons butter

Directions:

1. Take out the grill gate and crisper basket.
2. Set Ninja Foodi Grill to bake.
3. Set it to 390 degrees F.
4. Preheat by selecting "start".
5. Add the potatoes inside.
6. Seal and cook for 45 minutes.
7. Let cool.
8. Make slices on top of the potatoes.
9. Create a small hole.
10. Top with butter and cheese.
11. Put the potatoes back to the pot.
12. Bake at 375 degrees F for 10 minutes.
13. Top with sour cream and bacon before serving.

Cinnamon French Toast

Servings: 2
Cooking Time: 6 Minutes

Ingredients:

- 2 eggs
- ¼ cup whole milk
- 3 tablespoons sugar
- 2 teaspoons olive oil
- 1/8 teaspoon vanilla extract
- 1/8 teaspoon ground cinnamon
- 4 bread slices

Directions:

1. In a large bowl, mix all the ingredients except bread slices.
2. Coat the bread slices with egg mixture evenly.
3. Press the "Power Button" of Air Fry Oven and turn the dial to select the "Air Fry" mode.
4. Press the Time button and again turn the dial to set the cooking time to 6 minutes.
5. Now push the Temp button and rotate the dial to set the temperature at 390 degrees F.
6. Press the "Start/Pause" button to start.
7. When the unit beeps to show that it is preheated, open the lid and lightly grease the sheet pan.
8. Arrange the bread slices into "Air Fry Basket" and insert it in the oven.
9. Flip the bread slices once halfway through.
10. Serve warm.

DESSERTS RECIPES

Blondies

Servings: 4
Cooking Time: 15 Minutes

Ingredients:
- Cooking spray
- 6 tablespoons butter, melted
- 2 egg yolks
- 1 cup brown sugar
- Salt to taste
- 1 teaspoon vanilla extract
- 1 teaspoon baking powder
- 1 cup all-purpose flour
- 1 cup butterscotch chips
- ½ cup pecans, diced

Directions:
1. Spray a small baking pan with oil.
2. In a bowl, mix the butter, egg yolks, brown sugar, salt and vanilla.
3. Stir in the baking powder and flour.
4. Fold in the flour and baking powder.
5. Pour into the pan.
6. Place the pan inside the unit.
7. Select bake function.
8. Bake at 320 degrees F for 15 to 20 minutes.

Coffee Flavored Doughnuts

Servings: 6
Cooking Time: 6 Minutes

Ingredients:

- Baking powder 1 tsp.
- Salt ½ tsp.
- Sunflower oil 1 tbsp.
- Coffee ¼ cup
- Coconut sugar ¼ cup
- White all-purpose flour 1 cup
- Aquafaba 2 tbsp

Directions:

1. Combine sugar, flour, baking powder, salt in a mixing bowl.
2. In another bowl, combine the aquafaba, sunflower oil, and coffee.
3. Mix to form a dough.
4. Let the dough rest inside the fridge.
5. Preheat the air fryer to 400°F.
6. Knead the dough and create doughnuts.
7. Arrange inside the air fryer in a single layer and cook for 6 minutes.
8. Do not shake so that the donut maintains its shape.

Easter Tsoureki

Servings: Up To 8 People
Cooking Time: 30 - 45

Ingredients:

- flour 0: 500 gr
- fresh yeast: 20 gr
- milk: 125 ml
- eggs: 2
- sugar: 50 gr
- oranges: 2
- butter at room temperature: 75 gr
- mahlepi: 2 spoons
- warm water: 100 ml
- Red colored boiled eggs: 3

Directions:

1. Pour the flour into a bowl, form a hole in the center and add all the other ingredients (keep only the boiled eggs aside).
2. Knead well with your hands until you get a smooth and soft dough with which you will form a ball that you will leave to rise in a bowl sprinkled with flour on the bottom. Cover with a clean cloth and store in a warm place away from drafts.
3. In the meantime cook the eggs in water for 9 min from the moment of boiling and once cooled color them red following the instructions on the color pack.
4. Remove the stirrer blade from the tank.
5. After about 1 h of leavening take the dough and divide it into 3 pieces; roll each piece into a cylinder of about 45 cm and start to form a braid. Then join the ends to form a crown that will be placed inside the previously buttered tank.
6. Place the 3 cooled eggs on top of the crown and brush the dough with egg yolk.
7. Close the lid, select the BAKE program, power level 2, set 35min and press the program start/stop button.
8. After baking, cool the bread and serve with butter.

Butter Cake

Servings: 6
Cooking Time: 12 Minutes

Ingredients:

- 14 oz. cookie butter
- 3 eggs, beaten
- ¼ cup granulated sugar
- Cooking spray

Directions:

1. Microwave cookie butter for 90 seconds, stirring every 30 seconds.
2. In a bowl, add the cookie butter, eggs and sugar.
3. Spray a small baking pan with oil.
4. Pour the batter onto the baking pan.
5. Air fry at 320 degrees F for 10 minutes.

Cream And Pine Nuts Tart

Servings: Up To 10 People
Cooking Time: 45 -60

Ingredients:

- flour: 250 gr
- butter: 125 gr
- sugar: 110 gr
- eggs (1 whole and 1 yolk): 2
- salt: q.b.
- custard cream: 500m

Directions:

1. Put in the mixer the flour, sugar, eggs, butter just removed from the refrigerator and cut into chunks and a pinch of salt.
2. Blend everything until the dough is compact and elastic enough. Put everything to rest in the refrigerator for at least half an hour.
3. Remove the mixer blade from the bowl.
4. Butter and flour the bottom well. Spread the shortcrust pastry at a thickness of 3-4 mm and place it in the bottom of the tank covering the edge well.
5. Prick the bottom with the tines of a fork and spread the custard over it, leveling it with a spoon.
6. Finish the tart by covering it all with pine nuts.
7. Close the lid, select the BAKE program, set 55min and press the program start/stop button.
8. Let the pie cool well before turning it upside down.

Chocolate Brownies

Servings: 4
Cooking Time: 15 Minutes

Ingredients:
- ½ cup all-purpose flour
- ¾ cup sugar
- 6 tablespoons unsweetened cocoa powder
- ¼ teaspoon baking powder
- ¼ teaspoon salt
- ¼ cup unsalted butter, melted
- 2 large eggs
- 1 tablespoon vegetable oil
- ½ teaspoon vanilla extract

Directions:
1. Grease a 7-inch baking pan generously. Set aside.
2. In a bowl, add all the ingredients and mix until well combined.
3. Place the mixture into the prepared baking pan, and with the back of a spoon, smooth the top surface.
4. Arrange the drip pan at the bottom of the Instant Ninja Foodi Plus Air Fryer Oven cooking chamber.
5. Select "Air Fry" and then adjust the temperature to 330 degrees F.
6. Set the timer for 15 minutes and press the "Start."
7. When the display shows "Add Food," place the baking pan over the drip pan.
8. When the display shows "Turn Food," do nothing.
9. When cooking time is complete, remove the pan from the Ninja Foodi and place onto a wire rack to cool completely before cutting.
10. Cut the brownie into desired-sized squares and serve.

Original French Pineapple Toast

Servings: 4
Cooking Time: 16 Minutes

Ingredients:
- 10 bread slices
- ¼ cup of sugar
- ¼ cup milk
- 3 large whole eggs
- 1 cup of coconut milk
- 10 slices pineapple, peeled
- ½ cup coconut flakes
- Cooking spray as needed

Directions:
1. Take a mixing bowl and whisk in coconut milk, sugar, eggs, milk and stir well
2. Dup breads in the mixture and keep the mon the side for 2 minutes
3. Preheat Ninja Foodi by pressing the "GRILL" option and setting it to "MED" and timer to 16 minutes
4. Let it preheat until you hear a beep
5. Arrange bread slices over the grill grate, lock lid, and cook for 2 minutes. Flip and cook for 2 minutes more, let them cook until the timer reads 0
6. Repeat with remaining slices, serve, and enjoy!

Fudge Brownies

Servings: 6

Cooking Time: 1 Hour

Ingredients:

- 1/2 cup all-purpose flour
- Pinch salt
- 1/4 cup cocoa powder
- 2 eggs
- 1/2 cup brown sugar
- 1/2 cup white sugar
- 1 tablespoon vanilla extract
- 1 tablespoon water
- 3/4 cup butter, melted
- 6 oz. chocolate chips, melted

Directions:

1. Combine flour, salt and cocoa powder in a bowl.
2. Beat eggs in another bowl.
3. Stir in sugars, vanilla and water.
4. Add butter and chocolate chips to the mixture.
5. Slowly add dry ingredients to this mixture.
6. Mix well.
7. Spray small baking pan with oil.
8. Pour batter into the pan.
9. Add crisper plate to the air fry basket in the Ninja Foodi Grill.
10. Choose air fry setting.
11. Preheat at 300 degrees F for 3 minutes.
12. Add small baking pan to the crisper plate.
13. Cook for 1 hour.

Cheesy Cauliflower Steak

Servings: 4

Cooking Time: 30 Minutes

Ingredients:

- 1 tablespoon mustard
- 1 head cauliflower
- 1 teaspoon avocado mayonnaise
- ½ cup parmesan cheese, grated
- ¼ cup butter, cut into small pieces

Directions:

1. Set your Ninja Foodi to Sauté mode, and add butter and cauliflower.
2. Sauté for 3 minutes.
3. Add remaining ingredients and stir.
4. Lock the lid and cook on High pressure for 30 minutes.
5. Release pressure naturally over 10 minutes.
6. Serve and enjoy!

Mozzarella Sticks And Grilled Eggplant

Servings: 4

Cooking Time: 14 Minutes

Ingredients:

- Salt as needed
- ½ pound buffalo mozzarella, sliced into ¼-inch thick
- 12 large basil leaves
- 2 heirloom tomatoes, sliced into ¼ inch thickness
- 2 tablespoon canola oil
- 1 eggplant, ¼-inch thick

Directions:

1. Take a large bowl and add the eggplant, add oil and toss well until coated well.
2. Preheat your Ninja Foodi to MAX and set the timer to 15 minutes.
3. Once you hear the beeping sound, transfer the prepared eggplants to your Grill and cook for 8-12 minutes until the surface is charred.
4. Top with cheese slice, tomato, and mozzarella.
5. Cook for 2 minutes, letting the cheese melt.
6. Remove from grill and place 2-3 basil leaves on top of half stack.
7. Place remaining eggplant stack on top alongside basil.
8. Season well with salt and the rest of the basil.
9. Enjoy!

Fried Cream

Servings: Up To 8 People
Cooking Time: 15 - 30

Ingredients:

- Whole milk: 500mL
- Egg yolks: n.3
- Sugar: 150g
- Flour: 50g
- Vanillin: n.1 sachet
- Eggs: n.2
- Breadcrumbs: q.b.
- Oil: liv.4

Directions:

1. First prepare the custard; once cooked, pour it into a baking pan previously covered with transparent film and level it well; let it cool at room temperature for about 2 hours.
2. Remove the mixing paddle from the bowl.
3. Pour the oil into the tank and distribute it well over the entire bottom.
4. When the cream is cold, transfer it to a chopping board and cut it into cubes; pass each piece of cream first in the breadcrumbs, covering it well on all sides, then in the beaten egg and finally in the breadcrumbs.
5. Place each piece inside the tub, select the BAKE program, set 12min and press the program start/stop key.
6. Rotate the cream 1-2 times during cooking to even out the external browning.
7. With the doses of this cream you will have to do 2/3 cooking in sequence.

Lava Cake

Servings:4
Cooking Time: 15 Minutes

Ingredients:

- 6 ½ (1 ounce) squares of semisweet chocolate, should be finely chopped
- 3 eaches of eggs, at room temperature
- ½ cup of flour, should be cut into 8 pieces
- 4 teaspoons of unsweetened cocoa
- 2 tablespoons of all-purpose flour
- 1/3 cup of white sugar
- 1 pinch of salt

Directions:

1. Preheat your oven to 4000F (2000C). Then, grease and apply flour to 6-ounce of ramekins
2. Put the butter and chocolate at the top of a double boiler over simmering water. Stir as frequently as possible and use a rubber spatula to scrape down the sides to avoid scorching until the chocolate melts in about 5 minutes.
3. Combine sugar and egg in a large bowl, then beat with an electric mixer until it becomes pale and thick in about 5 minutes. Mix in cocoa powder, melted chocolate, and the flour until they all combine. Pour batter in your prepared ramekins and put on a baking tray.
4. Next is to bake in the preheated oven until the sides are set but the middle remains jiggly in 10-13 minutes. Let it cool for approximately 5 minutes before you serve.

Caramelized Pineapple Sundaes With Coconut

Servings: 10

Cooking Time: 30 Min

Ingredients:

- 1 - pineapple
- 2 tsp. vegetable oil
- ½ c. sweetened shredded coconut
- 2½ pt. fat-free vanilla frozen yogurt
- Mint sprigs

Directions:

1. Switch on Ninja Foodi broil. Brush the pineapple jewelry with the vegetable oil. Ninja Foodi oven broil over modestly high warm temperature, turning every so often till the pineapple is daintily roasted and mollified, approximately 8MIN. Move the jewelry to a work surface and reduce into reduced down portions.

2. In a medium skillet, toast the coconut over slight warmth until awesome, about 2MIN. Move to a plate to chill.

3. Scoop the yogurt into dessert glasses or bowls. Top with the Ninja Foodi oven-broiled pineapple, sprinkles with the coconut, adorn with the Mint twigs, and serve at once.

Marshmallow Banana Boat

Servings: 4
Cooking Time: 6 Minutes

Ingredients:

- ½ cup peanut butter chips
- 1/3 cup chocolate chips
- 1 cup mini marshmallow
- 4 ripe bananas

Directions:

1. Take the banana and slice them gently, keeping the peel
2. Make sure to not cut it all the way through
3. Use your hands to carefully peel the banana skin like a book, revealing the banana flesh
4. Divide your marshmallow, peanut butter, chocolate chips among the prepared bananas, stuff them well
5. Preheat your Grill in "MEDIUM" mode, with the timer set to 6 minutes
6. Once you hear a beep, transfer your prepared bananas to the grill grate, cook for   6 minutes until the chocolate melts well
7. Serve and enjoy!

Rois Crackers

Servings: Up To 8 People
Cooking Time: 30 - 45

Ingredients:
- Puff pastry: n.2
- Almond flour: 100g
- Egg: n.1
- Sugar: 75g
- Butter: 50g
- Almond flavor: n.1 vial
- Porcelain bean: n.1

Directions:
1. First prepare the filling:
2. Mix the flour, egg, sugar, butter at room temperature and almond extract in a bowl.
3. Remove the mixing paddle from the bowl.
4. Roll out a sheet of pastry with baking paper underneath the bowl; prick it with a fork and stuff with the filling; roll out well.
5. Place the bean inside, choosing an external position for the cake.
6. Cover with the second roll of pastry and seal the edges well; brush the surface with a yolk diluted with milk and make decorative incisions.
7. Close the cover, select BAKE program, power level 2, set 35min and press program start/stop button.
8. Tradition has it that whoever happens to have the object hidden in his piece of cake, is considered the king of the day.

MEAT RECIPES

Turkey Burgers

Servings: 8 Burgers
Cooking Time: 12 Mins

Ingredients:
- 2 pounds of minced turkey
- 1/2 cup breadcrumbs
- 2 tbsp mustard
- 2 eggs
- Salt and pepper to taste
- Tomatoes, lettuce, onions, and sauce for burger garnish as preferred.

Directions:
1. Place your Ninja Foodi grill grate in the unit and close the hood. Choose GRILL, set temperature to MAX, and set time to 12 minutes. Select START/STOP to start your pre-heating.
2. Mix all ingredients with the turkey mince until combined.
3. When pre-heating is done, shape four large patties and place them into the grill. Close the hood and cook for twelve minutes, flipping halfway through.
4. Warm the buns on the grill or in the oven or microwave if preferred
5. Serve with toppings to taste.

Roast Beef With Chimichurri

Servings: 6

Cooking Time: 30 Minutes

Ingredients:

- 2 lb. roast beef
- 2 tablespoons olive oil
- Salt and pepper to taste
- Chimichurri
- ¼ cup olive oil
- ½ cup cilantro
- ½ cup parsley
- 2 tablespoons fresh oregano, sliced
- ¼ red wine vinegar
- 2 cloves garlic, minced
- Salt and pepper to taste

Directions:

1. Preheat your unit by pressing air crisp.
2. Press start.
3. Preheat for 4 minutes.
4. Brush roast beef with oil.
5. Season with salt and pepper.
6. Select roast function.
7. Cook at 250 degrees F for 3 hours.
8. Add all the ingredients to a food processor.
9. Pulse until smooth.
10. Serve the roast beef with chimichurri.

Bacon Wrapped Pork Tenderloin

Servings: 4
Cooking Time: 12 Minutes

Ingredients:

- 8 slices bacon
- 4 pork tenderloin fillets
- 2 tablespoons vegetable oil
- Salt and pepper to taste

Directions:

1. Wrap pork tenderloin with 2 bacon slices.
2. Secure with toothpicks.
3. Brush all sides with oil.
4. Season with salt and pepper.
5. Select grill function.
6. Choose high setting.
7. Set it to 12 minutes.
8. Press start.
9. After preheating the unit, add pork to the grill grate.
10. Cook for 6 minutes per side.

Chicken, Potatoes & Cabbage

Servings: 8
Cooking Time: 40 Minutes

Ingredients:

- 1 cup apple cider vinegar
- 2 lb. chicken thigh fillets
- 6 oz. barbecue sauce
- 2 lb. cabbage, sliced into wedges and steamed
- 1 lb. potatoes, roasted
- Salt and pepper to taste

Directions:

1. Pour apple cider vinegar to the inner pot.
2. Add grill grate to the Ninja Foodi Grill.
3. Place the chicken on top of the grill.
4. Sprinkle both sides with salt and pepper.
5. Grill the chicken for 15 to 20 minutes per side at 350 degrees F.
6. Baste the chicken with the barbecue sauce.
7. Serve chicken with potatoes and cabbage.

Pear Fresh Pork

Servings: 6
Cooking Time: 12 Minutes

Ingredients:

- 2 pounds pork tenderloin, ¾ inch slices
- 2 garlic cloves, minced
- 1 1/2 teaspoons ground cumin
- 1 1/2 teaspoons dried oregano
- 1/2 teaspoon black pepper
- 1/4 cup lime juice
- 2 tablespoons olive oil
- Pear Mix:
- 1 jalapeno pepper, seeded and chopped
- 2 tablespoons lime juice
- 4 cups pears, chopped peeled
- 1 teaspoon sugar
- 1/3 cup chopped red onion
- 2 tablespoons chopped mint
- 1 tablespoon lime zest, grated
- 1/2 teaspoon black pepper

Directions:

1. Season the pork with lime juice, cumin, oregano, oil, garlic, and pepper in a bowl. Cover and refrigerate for 8 hours or overnight to marinate.
2. In a mixing bowl, add the pear mix ingredients. Combine the ingredients to mix well with each other.
3. Take Ninja Foodi Grill, arrange it over your kitchen platform, and open the top lid. Arrange the grill grate and close the top lid.
4. Press "GRILL" and select the "HIGH" grill function. Adjust the timer to 12 minutes and then press "START/STOP." Ninja Foodi will start preheating.
5. Ninja Foodi is preheated and ready to cook when it starts to beep. After you hear a beep, open the top lid. Arrange the pork slices over the grill grate.
6. Close the top lid and cook for 6 minutes. Now open the top lid, flip the pork slices.
7. Close the top lid and cook for 6 more minutes.
8. Serve the sliced pork warm with the pear mixture on top.

Classic Cookies With Hazelnuts

Servings: 6
Cooking Time: 10 Minutes

Ingredients:

- 1 cup almond flour
- 1/2 cup coconut flour
- 1 teaspoon baking soda
- 1 teaspoon fine sea salt
- 1 stick butter
- 1 cup swerve
- 2 teaspoons vanilla
- 2 eggs, at room temperature
- 1 cup hazelnuts, coarsely chopped

Directions:

1. Begin by preheating your air fryer to 350 degrees f.
2. Mix the flour with the baking soda, and sea salt.
3. In the bowl of an electric mixer, beat the butter, swerve, and vanilla until creamy. Fold in the eggs, one at a time, and mix until well combined.
4. Slowly and gradually, stir in the flour mixture. Finally, fold in the coarsely chopped hazelnuts.
5. Divide the dough into small balls using a large cookie scoop; drop onto the prepared cookie sheets. Bake for 10 minutes or until golden brown, rotating the pan once or twice through the cooking time.
6. Work in batches and cool for a couple of minutes before removing to wire racks and serve.

Beer Battered Fish And Chips

Servings: 8

Cooking Time: 25 Mins

Ingredients:

- For the fries -
- 1 ½ pound of potatoes
- Pinch of salt
- Vegetable oil to coat for frying
- For the fish –
- 3 pounds of fresh fish (cod or herring works best)
- 1 standard bottle light beer
- 2 ½ cups all-purpose flour
- Salt and pepper (about 1 tsp each)
- Dried rosemary, sage, and basil or similar herbs

Directions:

1. To make the fries –
2. Cut the potatoes into fry shapes about 1 inch thick
3. Rinse in a colander with cold water to clean off the starch and then pat dry
4. Place your Ninja Foodi crisper basket in the unit and close the hood. Choose AIR FRY and set it to 350 degrees. Select START/STOP to start your pre-heating.
5. After pre-heating, lightly coat fries with vegetable oil and cook in small batches for 15 mins. Alternatively, remove halfway through then refry at a slightly higher temperature for extra crisp.
6. Season the fresh fries with salt.
7. To make the fish –
8. Combine 1 ½ cups of flour with all seasonings and herbs
9. Whisk in the cold beer until just thinner than pancake batter.
10. Place your Ninja Foodi crisper basket in the unit and close the hood. Choose AIR FRY and set it to 350 to 375 degrees. Select START/STOP to start your pre-heating.
11. Toss fish in the remaining flour then dip in beer batter.
12. Fry a few at a time for 7 minutes, flipping halfway through.
13. Serve with fries, tartar sauce, lemon, and malt vinegar immediately.

Juiciest Keto Bacon Strips

Servings: 2
Cooking Time: 8 Minutes

Ingredients:

- 10 bacon strips
- 1/4 teaspoon chili flakes
- 1/3 teaspoon salt
- 1/4 teaspoon basil, dried

Directions:

1. Rub the bacon strips with chili flakes, dried basil, and salt
2. Turn on your air fryer and place the bacon on the rack
3. Lower the air fryer lid. Cook the bacon at 400F for 5 minutes
4. Cook for 3 minutes more if the bacon is not fully cooked. Serve and enjoy!

Deliciously Smothered Pork Chops

Servings: 4

Cooking Time: 28 Minutes

Ingredients:

- 6 ounce of boneless pork loin chops
- 1 tablespoon of paprika
- 1 teaspoon of garlic powder
- 1 teaspoon of onion powder
- 1 teaspoon of black pepper
- 1 teaspoon of salt
- ¼ teaspoon of cayenne pepper
- 2 tablespoon of coconut oil
- ½ of a sliced medium onion
- 6-ounce baby Bella mushrooms, sliced
- 1 tablespoon of butter
- ½ a cup of whip cream
- ¼ teaspoon of xanthan gum
- 1 tablespoon parsley, chopped

Directions:

1. Take a small bowl and add garlic powder, paprika, onion powder, black pepper, salt, and cayenne pepper.
2. Rinse the pork chops and pat them dry.
3. Sprinkle both sides with 1 teaspoon of the mixture, making sure to rub the seasoning all over the meat. Reserve the remaining spice.
4. Set your Ninja Foodi to Sauté and add coconut oil. Allow the oil to heat up.
5. Brown the chops, 3 minutes per side.
6. Remove and cancel the Sauté mode.
7. Add sliced onion to the base of your pot alongside mushrooms.
8. Top with the browned pork chops.
9. Lock the lid and cook on high pressure for 25 minutes.
10. Release the pressure naturally over 10 minutes. Remove the pork chops and keep them on a plate.
11. Set your pot to Sauté mode and whisk in remaining spices mix, heavy cream, and butter.
12. Sprinkle ¼ teaspoon of Xanthan gum and stir.
13. Simmer for 3-5 minutes and remove the heat.
14. Add a bit more Xanthan gum if you require a heavier gravy.
15. Top the pork chops with the gravy, and sprinkle parsley.

16. Serve!

Grilled Pork Chops

Servings: 4
Cooking Time: 15 Minutes

Ingredients:
- 4 pork chops
- Barbecue sauce
- Salt and pepper to taste

Directions:
1. Add grill grate to your Ninja Foodi Grill.
2. Set it to grill. Close the hood.
3. Preheat to high for 15 minutes.
4. Season pork chops with salt and pepper.
5. Add to the grill grates.
6. Grill for 8 minutes.
7. Flip and cook for another 7 minutes, brushing both sides with barbecue sauce.
8. Serving Suggestions: Let rest for 5 minutes before slicing and serving.

Beef, Pearl Onions And Cauliflower

Servings: 4
Cooking Time: 12 Minutes

Ingredients:

- 1 ½ pounds new york strip, cut into strips
- 1 (1-pound head cauliflower, broken into florets
- 1 cup pearl onion, sliced
- Marinade:
- 1 tablespoon olive oil
- 2 cloves garlic, minced
- 1 teaspoon of ground ginger
- 1/4 cup tomato paste
- 1/2 cup red wine

Directions:

1. Mix all ingredients for the marinade. Add the beef to the marinade and let it sit in your refrigerator for 1 hour.
2. Preheat your air fryer to 400 degrees f. Transfer the meat to the air fryer basket. Add the cauliflower and onions.
3. Drizzle a few tablespoons of marinade all over the meat and vegetables. Cook for 12 minutes, shaking the basket halfway through the cooking time. Serve warm.

Chili Dogs

Servings: 16
Cooking Time: 40 Mins

Ingredients:

- If making the chili -
- 1 ½ jar of pasta sauce
- 2 tsp of butter or margarine
- 2 pounds of ground beef
- At least 2 tsp chili powder
- 2 tsp vegetable oil
- 4 minced garlic cloves
- 1 white onion, finely chopped
- 2 tsp salt
- Also requires –
- Hot dog buns
- 2 tbsp butter
- 16 beef hot dogs

Directions:

1. Prepare the chili. If it is store-bought, follow instructions. If making fresh chili, heat the olive oil and butter in a skillet then fry the ground beef, garlic, and onions.
2. Use the back of a spoon to break it up and cook until browning before adding the other ingredients. Simmer for 15 mins.
3. Place your Ninja Foodi grill grate in the unit and close the hood. Choose GRILL, set temperature to MAX, and set time to 10 minutes. Select START/STOP to start your pre-heating.
4. When the pre-heating timer goes off, place the hot dogs on the grill grate, close the hood, and cook for 3-5 mins. Flip halfway through.
5. Butter the buns. They can also be heated on the grill, oven, or microwave as you like.
6. Put the dogs in buns and top with chili and your other favorite toppings.

Herb-roasted Chicken

Servings: 4
Cooking Time: 5 Hours

Ingredients:

- 1 whole chicken
- 5 cloves garlic, crushed
- 1 tablespoon canola oil
- ¼ cup lemon juice
- ¼ cup honey
- 5 sprigs thyme, chopped
- 2 tablespoons salt
- 1 tablespoon pepper

Directions:

1. Add garlic inside the chicken cavity.
2. Brush all sides of chicken with mixture of oil, lemon juice and honey.
3. Sprinkle with thyme, salt and pepper.
4. Place inside the unit.
5. Choose roast.
6. Cook at 250 degrees F for 5 hours.

Beef Chops With English Mustard And Coriander

Servings: 3
Cooking Time: 27 Minutes

Ingredients:

- 1 ½ teaspoon english mustard
- 3 boneless beef chops
- 1/3 teaspoon garlic pepper
- 2 teaspoons oregano, dried
- 2 tablespoons vegetable oil
- 1 ½ tablespoons fresh coriander, chopped
- 1/2 teaspoon onion powder
- 1/2 teaspoon basil, dried
- Grated rind of 1/2 small-sized lime
- 1/2 teaspoon fine sea salt

Directions:

1. Firstly, make the rub for the beef chops by mixing all the ingredients, except the chops and the new potatoes.
2. Now, evenly spread the beef chops with the english mustard rub.
3. Then, arrange the new potatoes in the bottom of the air fryer cooking basket. Top them with the prepared beef chops.
4. Roast for about 27 minutes at 365 degrees f, turning halfway through. Serve on individual plates with a keto salad on the side, if desired.

Panko Chicken Breast

Servings: 2
Cooking Time: 15 Minutes

Ingredients:

- 1 large egg, beaten
- 1/4 cup flour, preferably all-purpose
- 3/4 cup panko bread crumbs
- 1/3 cup Parmesan, freshly grated
- 2 tsp lemon zest
- 1 tsp dried oregano
- 1/2 tsp cayenne pepper
- Salt
- Black pepper
- 2 chicken breasts, boneless skinless

Directions:

1. Beat eggs in one bowl and spread the flour in another shallow bowl.
2. Whisk panko with cayenne, salt, black pepper, oregano, lemon zest, and parmesan in a shallow tray.
3. Take the chicken breasts and coat them with flour, then dip in eggs.
4. Coat the chicken breasts with the panko mixture and place them in the Air Fryer.
5. Place this Air Fryer inside the Ninja Foodi Oven and Close its lid.
6. Rotate the Ninja Foodi dial to select the "Air Fry" mode.
7. Press the Time button and again use the dial to set the cooking time to 10 minutes.
8. Now press the Temp button and rotate the dial to set the temperature at 350 degrees F.
9. Flip the chicken and return to cooking for another 5 minutes on the same mode and temperature.
10. Serve warm.

POULTRY RECIPES

Delicious Maple Glazed Chicken

Servings: 4
Cooking Time: 15 Minutes

Ingredients:

- 2 pounds chicken wings, bone-in
- 1 teaspoon black pepper, ground
- ¼ cup teriyaki sauce
- 1 cup maple syrup
- 1/3 cup soy sauce
- 3 garlic cloves, minced
- 2 teaspoons garlic powder
- 2 teaspoons onion powder

Directions:

1. Take a mixing bowl, add garlic, soy sauce, black pepper, maple syrup, garlic powder, onion powder, and teriyaki sauce, combine well
2. Add the chicken wings and combine well to coat
3. Arrange the grill grate and close the lid
4. Pre-heat Ninja Foodi by pressing the "GRILL" option and setting it to "MED" and timer to 10 minutes
5. Let it pre-heat until you hear a beep
6. Arrange the chicken wings over the grill grate lock lid and cook for 5 minutes
7. Flip the chicken and close the lid, cook for 5 minutes more
8. Cook until it reaches 165 degrees F
9. Serve warm and enjoy!

Baked Coconut Chicken

Servings: 4
Cooking Time: 12 Minutes

Ingredients:

- 2 large eggs
- 2 teaspoons garlic powder
- 1 teaspoon salt
- ½ teaspoon ground black pepper
- ¾ cup coconut aminos
- 1-pound chicken tenders
- Cooking spray as needed

Directions:

1. Pre-heat Ninja Foodi by squeezing the "AIR CRISP" alternative and setting it to "400 Degrees F" and timer to 12 minutes
2. Take a large-sized baking sheet and spray it with cooking spray
3. Take a wide dish and add garlic powder, eggs, pepper, and salt
4. Whisk well until everything is combined
5. Add the almond meal and coconut and mix well
6. Take your chicken tenders and dip them in the egg followed by dipping in the coconut mix
7. Shake off any excess
8. Transfer them to your Ninja Foodi Grill and spray the tenders with a bit of oil.
9. Cook for 12-14 minutes until you have a nice golden-brown texture
10. Enjoy!

Exotic Pilaf Chicken

Servings: 4
Cooking Time: 15 Minutes

Ingredients:

- 1 tablespoon unsalted butter
- 4 boneless, skin-on chicken thighs
- 1 ¾ cups water
- 1 tablespoon extra-virgin olive oil
- 1 teaspoon garlic powder
- 1 (6-ounce) box rice pilaf
- 1 teaspoon kosher salt

Directions:

1. Take Ninja Foodi multi-cooker, arrange it over a cooking platform, and open the top lid.
2. In the pot, add water, butter, and pilaf, and place a reversible rack inside the pot. Place the chicken thighs over the rack.
3. Seal the multi-cooker by locking it with the pressure lid, ensure to keep the pressure release valve locked/sealed.
4. Select "PRESSURE" mode and select the "HI" pressure level. Then after, set timer to 4 minutes and press "STOP/START," it will start the cooking process by building up inside pressure.
5. When the timer goes off, quickly release pressure by adjusting the pressure valve to the VENT. After pressure gets released, open the pressure lid.
6. In a mixing bowl, combine together the olive oil, salt, and garlic powder. Brush thickens with this mixture.
7. Seal the multi-cooker by locking it with the Crisping Lid, ensure to keep the pressure release valve locked/sealed.
8. Select "BROIL" mode and select the "HI" pressure level. Then after, set timer to 10 minutes and press "STOP/START," it will start the cooking process by building up inside pressure.
9. When the timer goes off, quickly release pressure by adjusting the pressure valve to the VENT. After pressure gets released, open the Crisping Lid. Serve warm the chicken with cooked pilaf.

Peanut Chicken

Servings: 4
Cooking Time: 20 Minutes

Ingredients:

- 1½ lb. chicken breast, sliced into cubes
- Salt to taste
- 1 teaspoon oil
- 3 clove garlic, chopped
- 1 tablespoon ginger, chopped
- 13 oz. coconut milk
- 3 tablespoons soy sauce
- 3 tablespoons honey
- 2 tablespoons fresh lime juice
- 1 tablespoon chili garlic paste
- ½ cup peanut butter

Directions:

1. Season the chicken with salt. Set the Ninja Foodi to Sauté. Add the oil.
2. Cook the garlic and ginger for 1 minute.
3. Add the chicken and all the other ingredients except the peanut butter.
4. Mix well. Put the peanut butter on top of the chicken but do not stir.
5. Seal the pot. Set it to Pressure. Cook at high pressure for 9 minutes.
6. Release the pressure naturally.
7. serving Suggestions:
8. Serve on top of spinach leaves.

A Genuine Hassel Back Chicken

Servings: 4
Cooking Time: 60 Minutes

Ingredients:
- 4 tablespoons butter
- Salt and pepper to taste
- 2 cups fresh mozzarella cheese, thinly sliced
- 8 large chicken breasts
- 4 large Roma tomatoes, thinly sliced

Directions:
1. Make a few deep slits in chicken breasts, and season with salt and pepper.
2. Stuff mozzarella cheese slices and tomatoes in chicken slits.
3. Grease Ninja Foodi pot with butter and arrange stuffed chicken breasts.
4. Lock the lid and Bake/Roast for 1 hour at 365°F. Serve and enjoy!

Hearty Chicken Zucchini Kabobs

Servings: 4
Cooking Time: 15 Minutes

Ingredients:

- 1-pound chicken breast, boneless, skinless and cut into cubes of 2 inches
- ¼ cup extra-virgin olive oil
- 2 tablespoons oregano
- 2 tablespoons Greek yogurt, plain
- 4 lemons juice
- 1 red onion, quartered
- 1 zucchini, sliced
- 1 lemon zest
- ½ teaspoon ground black pepper
- 4 garlic cloves, minced
- 1 teaspoon of sea salt

Directions:

1. Take a mixing bowl, add the Greek yogurt, lemon juice, oregano, garlic, zest, salt, and pepper, combine them well
2. Add the chicken and coat well, refrigerate for 1-2 hours to marinate
3. Arrange the grill grate and close the lid
4. Pre-heat Ninja Foodi by pressing the "GRILL" option and setting it to "MED" and timer to 7 minutes
5. Take the skewers, thread the chicken, zucchini and red onion and thread alternatively
6. Let it pre-heat until you hear a beep
7. Arrange the skewers over the grill grate lock lid and cook until the timer reads zero
8. Baste the kebabs with a marinating mixture in between
9. Take out your when it reaches 165 degrees F
10. Serve warm and enjoy!

Mexico's Favorite Chicken Soup

Servings: 4
Cooking Time: 20 Minutes

Ingredients:

- 2 cups chicken, shredded
- 4 tablespoons olive oil
- ½ cup cilantro, chopped
- 8 cups chicken broth
- 1/3 cup salsa
- 1 teaspoon onion powder
- ½ cup scallions, chopped
- 4 ounces green chilies, chopped
- ½ teaspoon habanero, minced
- 1 cup celery root, chopped
- 1 teaspoon cumin
- 1 teaspoon garlic powder
- Salt and pepper to taste

Directions:

1. Add all ingredients to Ninja Foodi. Stir and lock the lid. Cook on high pressure for 10 minutes.
2. Release pressure naturally over 10 minutes. Serve and enjoy!

Turkey Burrito

Servings: 2
Cooking Time: 8 Minutes

Ingredients:

- 4 slices turkey breast already cooked
- ½ red bell pepper, sliced
- 2 eggs
- 1 small avocado, peeled, pitted, and sliced
- 2 tablespoons salsa
- Salt and black pepper to the taste
- 1/8 cup mozzarella cheese, grated
- Tortillas for serving

Directions:

1. In a bowl, whisk eggs with salt and pepper to the taste, pour them in a pan and place it in the air fryer's basket.
2. Cook at 400 degrees F for 5 minutes, take the pan out of the fryer, and transfer eggs to a plate.
3. Roll your burritos and place them in your air fryer after you've lined it with some tin foil.
4. Heat the burritos at 300 degrees F for 3 minutes, divide them among plates and serve.
5. Enjoy!

Mexican Chicken Soup

Servings: 6
Cooking Time: 15 Min

Ingredients:

- 1 (14.5 ounces) can black beans, rinsed and drained
- 14 ounces canned whole tomatoes, chopped
- 5 chicken thighs, boneless, skinless
- 5 cups chicken broth
- 2 cups corn kernels
- ¼ cup cheddar cheese, shredded
- 2 tablespoon tomato puree
- 1 tablespoon chili powder
- 1 tablespoon ground cumin
- ½ teaspoon dried oregano
- 2 stemmed jalapeno peppers, cored and chopped
- 3 cloves garlic, minced
- Fresh cilantro, chopped to garnish

Directions:

1. Take Ninja Foodi multi-cooker, arrange it over a cooking platform, and open the top lid.
2. In the pot, add the chicken, chicken stock, cumin, oregano, garlic, tomato puree, tomatoes, chili powder, and jalapeno peppers; stir the mixture.
3. Seal the multi-cooker by locking it with the pressure lid; ensure to keep the pressure release valve locked/sealed.
4. Select "PRESSURE" mode and select the "HI" pressure level. Then, set timer to 10 minutes and press "STOP/START"; it will start the cooking process by building up inside pressure.
5. At the point when the clock goes off, brisk discharge pressure by adjusting the pressure valve to the VENT. After pressure gets released, open the pressure lid.
6. Shred the chicken and include it back in the pot.
7. Select "SEAR/SAUTÉ" mode and select "MD: HI" pressure level; add the beans and corn and combine, stir-cook for 4 minutes.
8. Add the cilantro and cheese on top; serve warm.

Honey-mustard Chicken Tenders

Servings: 4
Cooking Time: 4 Minutes

Ingredients:

- ½ cup Dijon mustard
- 2 tablespoons honey
- 2 tablespoons olive oil
- 1 teaspoon freshly ground black pepper
- 2 pounds chicken tenders
- ½ cup walnuts

Directions:

1. Whisk together the mustard, honey, olive oil, and pepper in a medium bowl. Add the chicken and toss to coat.
2. Finely grind the walnuts by pulsing them in a food processor or putting them in a heavy-duty plastic bag and pounding them with a rolling pin or heavy skillet.
3. Insert the Grill Grate and close the hood. Select GRILL, set the temperature to HIGH, and set the time to 4 minutes. Select START/STOP to begin preheating.
4. Toss the chicken tenders in the ground walnuts to coat them lightly.
5. Grill the chicken tenders for about 4 minutes, until they have taken on grill marks and are cooked through. Serve hot, at room temperature, or refrigerate and serve cold.

Rosemary Chicken

Servings: 4
Cooking Time: 6 Minutes

Ingredients:

- ½ cup balsamic vinegar
- 2 tablespoons olive oil
- 2 rosemary sprigs, coarsely chopped
- 2 pounds boneless, skinless chicken breasts, pounded to a ½-inch thickness

Directions:

1. Combine the balsamic vinegar, olive oil, and rosemary in a shallow baking dish. Add the chicken breasts and turn to coat. Cover with plastic wrap and refrigerate for at least 30 minutes or overnight.
2. Insert the Grill Grate and close the hood. Select GRILL, set the temperature to HIGH, and set the time to 6 minutes. Select START/STOP to begin preheating.
3. When the unit beeps to signify it has preheated, place the s chicken breasts on the Grill Grate. Close the hood and cook for 6 minutes until they have taken on grill marks and are cooked through.

The Tarragon Chicken Meal

Servings: 4
Cooking Time: 5 Minutes

Ingredients:
- For Chicken
- 1 and ½ pounds chicken tenders
- Salt as needed
- 3 tablespoons tarragon leaves, chopped
- 1 teaspoon lemon zest, grated
- 2 tablespoons fresh lemon juice
- 2 tablespoons extra virgin olive oil
- For Sauce
- 2 tablespoons fresh lemon juice
- 2 tablespoons butter, salted
- ½ cup heavy whip cream

Directions:
1. Prepare your chicken by taking a baking dish and arranging the chicken over the dish in a single layer
2. Season generously with salt and pepper
3. Sprinkle chopped tarragon and lemon zest all around the tenders
4. Drizzle lemon juice and olive oil on top
5. Let them sit for 10 minutes
6. Drain them well
7. Insert Grill Grate in your Ninja Foodi Grill and set to HIGH temperature
8. Set timer to 4 minutes
9. Once you hear the beep, place chicken tenders in your grill grate
10. Let it cook for 3-4 minutes until cooked completely
11. Do in batches if needed
12. Transfer the cooked chicken tenders to a platter
13. For the sauce, take a small-sized saucepan
14. Add cream, butter and lemon juice and bring to a boil
15. Once thickened enough, pour the mix over chicken
16. Serve and enjoy!
17. Serve and enjoy once ready!

Hassel Back Chicken

Servings: 4
Cooking Time: 1 Hour

Ingredients:

- 8 large chicken breasts
- 2 cups fresh mozzarella cheese, thinly sliced
- 4 large Roma tomatoes, thinly sliced
- 4 tablespoons butter
- Salt and pepper to taste

Directions:

1. Add chicken breasts, season with salt and pepper to make deep slits
2. Stuff with mozzarella cheese slices and tomatoes in your chicken slits
3. Grease Ninja Foodi pot with butter
4. Arrange stuffed chicken breasts
5. Close the lid and BAKE/ROAST for 1 hour at 365 degrees F
6. Serve and enjoy!

Honey Teriyaki Chicken

Servings: 4
Cooking Time: 20 Minutes

Ingredients:

- 4 chicken breasts, sliced into strips
- 1 cup soy sauce
- ½ cup water
- 2/3 cup honey
- 2 teaspoons garlic, minced
- ½ cup rice vinegar
- ½ teaspoon ground ginger
- ¼ teaspoon crushed red pepper flakes
- 3 tablespoons corn starch dissolved in 3 tablespoons cold water

Directions:

1. Put the chicken inside the Ninja Foodi.
2. Add the rest of the ingredients except the corn starch mixture.
3. Put on the lid. Set it to Pressure. Cook at high pressure for 30 minutes.
4. Release the pressure naturally. Set it to Sauté.
5. Stir in the corn starch and simmer until the sauce has thickened.
6. serving Suggestions:
7. Garnish with sesame seeds and serve with fried rice.

Chicken Marsala

Servings: 4
Cooking Time: 25 Minutes

Ingredients:
- 4 chicken breasts, sliced into strips
- 1 teaspoon garlic powder
- Salt and pepper to taste
- 1/2 cup all-purpose flour
- 3 tablespoons butter
- 3 tablespoons olive oil
- 3 cloves garlic, minced
- 1 shallot, sliced thinly
- 8 oz. mushrooms
- 2/3 cup Marsala wine
- 2/3 cup chicken stock
- 1/2 cup heavy cream

Directions:
1. Season the chicken with garlic powder, salt, and pepper. Coat the chicken with flour.
2. Place the chicken on the Ninja Foodi basket. Put the basket inside the pot.
3. Seal the crisping lid. Set it to air crisp. Cook at 375 degrees F for 15 minutes.
4. Remove and set aside. Set the pot to sauté. Add the butter and oil.
5. Cook the garlic, shallot, and mushrooms. Pour in the wine and chicken broth.
6. Simmer for 10 minutes. Stir in the heavy cream.
7. Toss the chicken into the mixture. Serve.

SNACK & APPETIZER RECIPES

Homemade Fries

Servings: 6
Cooking Time: 45 Minutes

Ingredients:

- 1 lb. large potatoes, sliced into strips
- 2 tablespoons vegetable oil
- Salt to taste

Directions:

1. Toss potato strips in oil.
2. Add crisper plate to the air fryer basket inside the Ninja Foodi Grill.
3. Choose air fry function. Set it to 390 degrees F for 3 minutes.
4. Press start to preheat.
5. Add potato strips to the crisper plate.
6. Cook for 25 minutes.
7. Stir and cook for another 20 minutes.

Ranch Chicken Fingers

Servings: 4
Cooking Time: 20 Minutes

Ingredients:

- 2 lb. chicken breast fillet, sliced into strips
- 1 tablespoon olive oil
- 1 oz. ranch dressing seasoning mix
- 4 cups breadcrumbs
- Salt to taste

Directions:

1. Coat chicken strips with olive oil.
2. Sprinkle all sides with ranch seasoning.
3. Cover with foil and refrigerate for 1 to 2 hours.
4. In a bowl, mix breadcrumbs and salt.
5. Dredge the chicken strips with seasoned breadcrumbs.
6. Add crisper plate to the air fryer basket inside the Ninja Foodi Grill.
7. Choose air fry setting.
8. Set it to 390 degrees F.
9. Preheat for 3 minutes.
10. Add chicken strips to the crisper plate.
11. Cook for 15 to 20 minutes, flipping halfway through.

Garlic Mashed Potatoes

Servings: 4
Cooking Time: 8 Minutes

Ingredients:

- 2 lb. potatoes, sliced into cubes
- 6 cloves garlic, crushed
- 2/3 cup chicken stock
- Salt and pepper to taste
- 3 tablespoons butter, divided
- 1/4 cup sour cream
- 1/4 cup cream cheese

Directions:

1. Place the potatoes inside the Ninja Foodi.
2. Add the chicken stock, garlic, salt, pepper, and 1/2 tablespoon butter.
3. Seal the pot.
4. Set it to pressure.
5. Cook at high pressure for 8 minutes.
6. Release the pressure naturally.
7. Mash the potatoes and stir in the rest of the ingredients and the remaining butter.

Mozzarella Bites

Servings: 12
Cooking Time: 8 Minutes

Ingredients:

- 12 mozzarella strips
- ¼ cup butter, melted
- 1 cup breadcrumbs

Directions:

1. Dip mozzarella strips in butter.
2. Dredge with breadcrumbs.
3. Add the mozzarella strips to the air crisp tray.
4. Select air crisp setting.
5. Cook at 320 degrees F for 8 minutes, flipping once.

Mayo Zucchini Mix

Servings: 4
Cooking Time: 10 Minutes

Ingredients:

- 1 tablespoon avocado oil
- 1 pound zucchinis, roughly cubed
- 1 yellow onion, chopped
- 1 teaspoon turmeric powder
- 1 cup baby kale
- 2 tablespoons mayonnaise
- 2 tablespoons mustard
- 1 cup parmesan cheese, grated

Directions:

1. Heat up the air fryer with the oil at 360 degrees f, add the onion, zucchinis and turmeric and cook for 2 minutes.
2. Add the other ingredients, toss, cook for 8 minutes more, divide between plates and serve for breakfast right away.

Chicken Salad With Blueberry Vinaigrette

Servings: 4
Cooking Time: 14 Minutes

Ingredients:

- 2 boneless skinless chicken breasts, halves
- 1 tablespoon olive oil
- 1 garlic clove, minced
- 1/4 teaspoon salt
- 1/4 teaspoon pepper
- Vinaigrette:
- 1/4 cup olive oil
- 1/4 cup blueberry preserves
- 2 tablespoons balsamic vinegar
- 2 tablespoons maple syrup
- 1/4 teaspoon ground mustard
- 1/8 teaspoon salt
- Dash pepper
- Salads:
- 1 package (10 oz. salad greens
- 1 cup fresh blueberries
- 1/2 cup canned oranges
- 1 cup crumbled goat cheese

Directions:

1. First season the chicken liberally with garlic, salt, pepper and oil in a bowl.
2. Cover to refrigerate for 30 minutes margination.
3. Prepare and preheat the Ninja Foodi Grill on the medium temperature setting.
4. Once it is preheated, open the lid and place the chicken in the grill.
5. Cover the Ninja Foodi Grill's lid and grill on the "Grilling Mode" for 5-7 minutes per side until the internal temperature reaches 330 degrees F.
6. Toss the remaining ingredients for salad and vinaigrette in a bowl.
7. Slice the grilled chicken and serve with salad.

Chili Cheesy Fries

Servings: 6

Cooking Time: 14 Minutes

Ingredients:

- 1 package frozen French fry
- Salt and pepper to taste
- 15 oz. chili
- ½ cup cheese, shredded

Directions:

1. Add French fries to the air crisp tray.
2. Select air crisp setting.
3. Set temperature to 400 degrees.
4. Set time to 15 minutes.
5. Flip French fries halfway through cooking.
6. In a pan over medium heat, add the chili and cheese.
7. Spread mixture over the fries.

Baked Potato Rounds

Servings: 8
Cooking Time: 18 Minutes

Ingredients:

- 2 large potatoes, sliced into thick rounds
- Cooking spray
- Salt and pepper to taste
- 1 cup cheese, shredded
- 4 bacon slices, cooked crisp and crumbled

Directions:

1. Add the potatoes to the air crisp tray.
2. Spray the top part with oil.
3. Sprinkle with salt and pepper.
4. Select air crisp setting.
5. Air fry the potatoes at 370 degrees F for 7 to 8 minutes per side.
6. Remove from the unit.
7. Top each potato with cheese and bacon bits.
8. Air fry for another 2 minutes or until cheese has melted.

Naan Pizza

Servings: 1
Cooking Time: 5 Minutes

Ingredients:
- Cooking spray
- 1 naan bread
- ¼ cup pesto
- ½ cup baby spinach, cooked
- ½ cup cherry tomatoes, sliced in half
- 1 cup mozzarella cheese

Directions:
1. Spray your air crisp tray with oil.
2. Spread pesto on top of the naan bread.
3. Top with spinach and tomatoes.
4. Sprinkle cheese on top.
5. Add naan pizza to the air crisp tray.
6. Choose air crisp setting.
7. Cook at 350 degrees F for 7 minutes.

Crispy Pickles

Servings: 4
Cooking Time: 30 Minutes

Ingredients:

- 1 cup all-purpose flour
- 3 eggs
- 1 cup breadcrumbs
- Garlic salt to taste
- 12 dill pickle spears
- Cooking spray

Directions:

1. Dip pickles in flour, eggs and then in a mixture of breadcrumbs and garlic salt.
2. Arrange on a plate.
3. Place inside the freezer for 30 minutes.
4. Add crisper basket to the Ninja Foodi Grill.
5. Choose air fry function.
6. Add pickles to the basket.
7. Spray with oil.
8. Cook at 375 degrees F for 18 to 20 minutes.
9. Flip and cook for another 10 minutes.

Bacon Brussels Delight

Servings: 4
Cooking Time: 12 Minutes

Ingredients:

- 6 slices bacon, chopped
- 1-pound Brussels sprouts halved
- 1/2 teaspoon black pepper
- 1 tablespoon of sea salt
- 2 tablespoons olive oil, extra-virgin

Directions:

1. Take a mixing bowl and toss the Brussels sprouts, olive oil, bacon, salt, and black pepper
2. Arrange the crisping basket inside the pot
3. Preheat Ninja Foodi by squeezing the "AIR CRISP" setting at 390 degrees F and timer to 12 minutes
4. Let it preheat until you hear a beep
5. Arrange the Brussels sprout mixture directly inside the basket
6. Close the top lid and cook for 6 minutes, then shake the basket
7. Close the top lid and cook for 6 minutes more
8. Serve warm and enjoy!

Cheese Dredged Cauliflower Snack

Servings: 4

Cooking Time: 33 Minutes

Ingredients:

- 1 head cauliflower
- ¼ cup butter, cut into small pieces
- ½ cup parmesan cheese, grated
- 1 teaspoon avocado mayonnaise
- 1 tablespoon mustard

Directions:

1. Set your Ninja Foodi to Sauté mode and add butter and cauliflower
2. Sauté for 3 minutes
3. Add rest of the ingredients
4. Give it a nice stir
5. Close the lid
6. Cook on HIGH pressure for 30 minutes
7. Release pressure naturally over 10 minutes
8. Serve and enjoy!

Garlic Bread

Servings: 4
Cooking Time: 5 Minutes

Ingredients:

- 4 cloves roasted garlic, chopped
- ½ cup butter, melted
- 1 tablespoon fresh parsley, chopped
- 1 loaf Italian bread
- Salt to taste

Directions:

1. Mix the garlic, butter and parsley in a bowl.
2. Spread the mixture on the bread slices.
3. Place the bread inside the unit.
4. Choose air crisp setting.
5. Cook at 400 degrees F for 3 minutes.

Barbeque Chicken Egg Rolls

Servings: 6
Cooking Time: 5 Mins

Ingredients:

- 1 diced onion
- Vegetable oil for air frying
- 1 cup barbeque sauce
- ½ cup fresh spinach, finely chopped
- 1 chopped bell pepper
- Egg roll wrappers (pre-packed)
- 2 cups of cubed cooked chicken
- 1 cup sweetcorn
- 2 cups shredded cheese (any melting kind will do)
- ½ tsp salt
- ¼ tsp pepper

Directions:

1. Mix the chicken in the barbeque sauce until fully saturated. Leave to settle for an hour in the fridge.
2. Place your Ninja Foodi crisper basket in the unit and close the hood. Choose AIR FRY. Select START/STOP to start your pre-heating.
3. Combine herbs, vegetables, and chicken in a bowl. Add the rest of the ingredients and mix thoroughly.
4. Spoon two tbsp of mixture into the center of each egg roll wrapper and roll according to directions.
5. Lightly coat in vegetable oil.
6. Place a small batch in the air fryer and cook for 1-2 mins until golden brown, shaking the basket for an even crisp.
7. Serve with a dip of your choice.

Blueberry Hand Pies

Servings: 6
Cooking Time: 25 Minutes

Ingredients:

- 1 cup blueberries
- 2.5 tbsp caster sugar
- 1 tsp lemon juice
- 1 pinch salt
- 14 oz. refrigerated pie crust
- water
- vanilla sugar to sprinkle on top

Directions:

1. Toss the blueberries with salt, lemon juice, and sugar in a medium bowl.
2. Spread the pie crust into a round sheet and cut 6-4 inch circles out of it.
3. Add a tbsp of blueberry filling at the center of each circle.
4. Moisten the edges of these circles and fold them in half then pinch their edges together.
5. Press the edges using a fork to crimp its edges.
6. Place the handpieces in the Air Fryer and spray them with cooking oil.
7. Drizzle the vanilla sugar over the hand pies.
8. Transfer the hand pies on the Air Fryer to the Ninja oven and Close its lid.
9. Rotate the Ninja Foodi dial to select the "Air Fry" mode.
10. Press the Time button and again use the dial to set the cooking time to 25 minutes.
11. Now press the Temp button and rotate the dial to set the temperature at 400 degrees F.
12. Serve fresh.

OTHER FAVORITE RECIPES

Grinders Sauce And Peppers

Servings: 6 Serves
Cooking Time: 26 Minutes

Ingredients:
- 6 cheap sausages, like hot Italian or Bratwurst, four ounces each
- 1 white onion, peeled, 1-inch rings cut.
- As desired, kosher salt
- Black pepper ground, as desired.
- 2 bell peppers, seeds, and ribs removed in sections.
- 2 tablespoons of canola oil, split.
- 6 hot dogs.
- Terms, as requested.

Directions:
1. Add the grill to the machine and remove the hood. Set temperature to low, pick grill and set time to 26 minutes. To start preheating, select start/stop.
2. Toss bell peppers and onions with butter, salt, and black pepper while the machine is preheating.
3. If the device shows that it is preheated, place peppers and onions on the grill. Open the hood and cook without flipping for 12 minutes.
4. Move peppers and onions to a medium mixing bowl after 12 minutes. Close the hood and cook for 6 minutes on a grill grate.
5. Flip sausages after 6 minutes. Close the hood and cook 6 minutes longer.
6. Split the grilled onions into single rings and blend with the peppers.
7. Pull sausages from the grill after 6 minutes. Place the buns on the grill, cut-sided down. Close the hood and cook for 2 minutes.
8. When the cooking is done, spread the seasonings onto the buns, then put the sausages into the buns. Top each with peppers and onions liberally and serve.

Grilled Basil, Cheese Goat & Olive Mini Pizzas

Servings: 2 Serves

Cooking Time: 7 Minutes

Ingredients:

- 2 teaspoons. Seeds of the fennel, roughly chopped.
- 1 lb. Pizza pullover
- Kosher salt and black pepper, freshly made.
- Olive oil extra-virgin when washing
- 4 for the surface of work
- 14 Scratched, quartered Kalamata olives.
- The red pepper flakes crushed.
- 1-1/2 Sambuca Teaspoon, or Pernod
- Cut into 36 thin wedges (if the cheese crumbles, let it warm at room temperature) or a log of fresh goat cheese, cut into thin rounds.
- 18 Cherry tomatoes or grape tomatoes, cut in 1/4" cubes, discarded ends.

Directions:

1. Heat a medium-high gas grill or prepare a medium-hot charcoal fire with the coals benched to one side to provide a cooler grill area.
2. Roll out the pizza dough with a rolling pin on a well-floured surface till it is 1/8 inch thick. If the dough is very elastic and is rolling resistant, cover it with plastic and let it rest for 5 minutes or so. You might need to repeat this step several times before the dough is comfortable and ready to roll. Cut the dough into 18 rounds using a 3-inch ring cutter. Keep off the extra dough. Sprinkle with oil on the top of the dough and sprinkle with salt, pepper, and fennel seeds, pressing gently to ensure that they stick. Transfer the rounds fennel side up to a baking sheet.
3. Grill them fennel side down for 1 minute to work with half the pizzettas at a time. Check the pizzettas: Flatten them with a metal spatula if they've puffed up. Brush with oil on the floured sides (which face up). Grill for around 1 minute, until the bottom is well browned and crisp. If required, loosen with a metal spatula and return the pizzettas to the baking sheet, grilled side up.
4. Working easy, top each with 2 Bûcheron wedges, 3 pieces of olive, 3 slices of tomatoes and a pinch of red pepper flakes. Using a small spoon to sprinkle a few drops of sambuca or Pernod over each pizzetta.
5. Bring the pizzettas to the grill for medium heat gas or the cooler side of a grill for charcoal. Continue grilling, covered, for about 2 minutes, until the pizzettas are crisp and the cheese melts. Transfer to a plate and serve with the remaining rounds of dough while you repeat.

Stickers Pot

Servings: 6 Serves
Cooking Time: 21 Minutes

Ingredients:

- 1 cup of green cold, thinly sliced.
- 38 wrappers for pot sticker (or round wrappers).
- 3/4 cup of shiitake (approximately 4 mushrooms) mushrooms, finely chopped.
- 3 scallions, minced white and green pieces
- 3 tablespoons of vegetable oil, split.
- 2 fresh ginger tablespoons, hairy
- 1 kosher salt tablespoon.
- 2 tablespoons of low-sodium soy sauce plus 1/2 cup
- 3 garlic cloves, sliced, hacked.
- 1 3/4 cups of water, split.
- 1 pound of ground pork uncooked.

Directions:

1. In a large bowl, combine pork, chocolate, scallion, ginger, garlic, salt, and 2 tablespoons of soy sauce.
2. Lay the wrappers on a clean, dry surface and place in the middle of each one a small tablespoon of filling. In a small bowl, pour 1/4 cup of water. Spread a bit of water along half the wrapper's circumference using your finger or brush, fold over the wrappers and punch together with the edges into half a lunar form. Place the pot stickers on a flat layer on a dish, cover with plastic cover, and refrigerate until ready to cook.)
3. In the pot, place 1/2 cup of water. In the lower bowl, place the reversible rack and spray with the cooking spray. Make sure they sit flat in 1 layer and place a third of the pot sticks on the rack.
4. Assemble the pressure lid to ensure a vent position for the pressure release valve. Steam is selected and time set to 3 minutes. To start, select start/stop.
5. Take off the lid carefully when steaming is complete. Remove the rack from the pot and wipe off the rest of the water.
6. Choose sear/sauté and set to HI. To start, select start/stop. Place 1 tablespoon of oil in the pot and heat to glow. Use tongs, add pot stickers and cook, about 2 minutes per side, until browned and crisp on both sides. To turn off sear/sauté, select start/stop.
7. Repeat steps 3 to 6 with 2 batches of pot stickers remaining. (Any uncooked pot stickers can also be frozen up to 2 weeks. Freeze in one plate in a flat layer, and then transfer to an uncooked plastic bag.)
8. When the cooking is finished, add 1/2 cup of soy sauce to the mix.

Fruit Bowls

Servings: 2
Cooking Time: 10 Minutes

Ingredients:

- 1 cup heavy cream
- 1 tablespoon butter, soft
- 2 tablespoons sugar
- ½ cup walnuts, chopped
- 1 pear, cubed
- 1 apple, cored and cubed
- 1 mango, peeled and cubed
- 1 avocado, peeled and cubed

Directions:

1. In your air fryer's pan, combine the pear with the apple and the other ingredients, toss and cook at 360 degrees f for 10 minutes.
2. Divide into bowls and serve for breakfast.

Gazpacho Grilled-vegetable

Servings: 10 Serves
Cooking Time: 30 Minutes

Ingredients:

- 2 corn paws, husked.
- Unpeeled 2 big, cored, and quartered red bell peppers.
- 1/2 teaspoon of red pepper crushed.
- 2 big, cored, and quartered yellow bell peppers.
- 2 cups of tomato juice.
- 2 medium zucchini, by longitudinally cut.
- 1/2 centimeter thick, 1 large white onion, cut into 1/2 centimeter dome.
- 4 large cloves of garlic.
- 1 thinly sliced English cucumber.
- 2 cups vegetable oil. 2 cubs.
- Salt kosher and pepper freshly ground.
- 2 tablespoons of vinegar red wine.
- 1 1/2 tea cubes ground cumin.
- Clean orange juice 1/2 cup.
- 3 cups of citrus juice.
- 1/4 cup of coriander chopped.

Directions:

1. Power a barbecue. Place the cloves of garlic on a skewer. Clean the garlic gently, bell pepper, courgette, onion, and maize with vegetable oil and add salt and pepper to the season. Grill the vegetables over moderately high heat and regularly rotate for about ten minutes until they are lightly charred and crisp. Place the peppers in a pot, plastic cover, and let it steam for 10 minutes.

2. Remove the garlic cloves from the sprouts, peel, and transfer to a large cup. Split the charred corn kernels into the bowl with a large clamped knife. Peel and put in a bowl the peppers with courgette, onion, cumin, red pepper crushed, tomato juice, orange juice, lemon juice, and vinegar.

3. Puree the vegetable mixture in the blender or food processor for batches. In a clean tub, pour the gazpacho and season with salt and pepper. Cover and refrigerate for about 2 hours until chilled.

4. Remove the cilantro into the gazpacho just before serving. Place the soup in cups, add the cucumber and eat.

Carob, Raspberry, Raspberry And Chocolate

Servings: 6 Serves

Cooking Time: 30 Minutes

Ingredients:

- Cut 50 g of dark chocolate into pieces.
- 100 g of cocoa sugar.
- 1 tablespoon powder baking.
- 150 g flour of choice.
- A hundred ml of milk.
- 1 ovum.
- Extract 1 teaspoon of vanilla.
- 75 g of frozen frosts.
- 30 g paste of carob.

Directions:

1. Preheat the oven to 180°C and grass the pudding tins 4-6 x 150 ml.
2. Into the Ninja Kitchen Nutri ninja blender and whizz until smooth, place the meal, sugar, carob, baking powder, milk, egg, and vanilla. Remove the chocolate and the raspberries.
3. Spread the mixture between the tins to the top. Place the pudding tins onto a baking tray and bake in the oven for about 30 minutes.
4. Let the tins cool down for 10 minutes, then take a knife and put out the puddings. You may enjoy them warmly – but let them cool if you want the yogurt topping.
5. Beat the yogurt, carob powder, and maple syrup with each cooled pudding. Disperse over cocoa nibs and freeze-dried raspberries and enjoy!

Meat Oatmeal Raisin

Servings: 10 Serves
Cooking Time: 4 Hours

Ingredients:

- 1 cup of black grapes.
- 1/2 cup of fast-cooking oats.
- 1 cubicle of sugar.
- Active dry yeast 1 pack (1/4 ounce)
- 2 spoonful of vegetable oil.
- 1 kosher salt tablespoon.
- 1 cup of unbleached flour of bread
- 3/4 tablespoons of hot water (110-115 ° F)
- 1/2 cup of whole flour of wheat

Directions:

1. Place the water, sugar, and yeast in a small bowl. Allow 5 minutes to sit.
2. Put yeast mixture, butter, salt, flours, oats, and raisins along with BLEND on a single blade, approximately 20 seconds.
3. Remove the dough ball and place it in a mixing bowl filled with vegetable oil. Cover with plastic wrap and let it sit for 2 hours in a warm place until the dough has doubled.
4. Cover a loaf pan lightly with a cooking mist. Shake dough into a loaf and put it in a pot. Let rise for 2 hours or twice as large.
5. Preheat the oven to 350 ° F. Preheat. Bake to golden brown for 35 to 40 minutes. Cool before serving.

Cheeseburgers Pimento-jalapeño

Servings: 4 Serves

Cooking Time: 25 Minutes

Ingredients:

- 4 slices of tomato ripe.
- 3/4 cup sliced jalapeño pickled peppers.
- Cut into a 1-inch cube (see note) 1 1/2 pounds beef chuck.
- Kosher salt and black pepper freshly ground.
- 4 soft buns.
- 1 1/2 cups of iceberg shredded salad
- 1/2 small, thinly sliced, white or yellow onion
- 1 cup of Cheese Pimento.

Directions:

1. In the food processor, place pimento cheese. Pulse 6 to 8 short pulses until finely chopped. Move to a small bowl with a spatula and, if used for molding meat, wash the food processor bowl.

2. Grind with a meat grinder: Place a grinding pipe, feeding tube, frame, die, and dust a meat grinder with a large blender in the freezer. Spread the beef chunks uniformly over a large platform or rimmed bakery in one sheet. Place meat in a freezer and freeze until the edges become firm, but still meltable for about 20 minutes. Set up a 3/8-inch meat grinder. In the cold bowl, grind beef. Fast working, grind meat with 1/4 inch plate. When grinder or meat gets too hot during grinding, return to freezer for 10 minutes before grinding.

3. To grind with a food processor, Spread beef chunks on a large platform or rimmed baking sheet evenly in a single layer. Place in a freezer and freeze until it gets solid, but still going, for approximately 20 minutes. Place meat cubes in a food processor's work bowl in three batches. Pulse, around 15 to 20 short pulses, until finely chopped. Transfer to a bowl with the remainder of the beef and repeat.

4. Former beef into four patties roughly 1/2 "wider than burger buns with moderate depression in the middle to cover the bulging when cooking. Apply salt and pepper generously and cool until ready to cook.

5. Light one charcoal-filled chimney. When the entire charcoal is lit and coated with grey ash, stretch the charcoal uniformly on one side. Instead, position half the gas grill burners at high temperatures. Put the cooking grill in place and cover with the grill and allow for 5 minutes to preheat. Wash the grilling grill and grease. Place burgers directly over hot coals, cover with open wind, and cook until well charred and centre of burgers record 110 ° F in instant thermometer read, approximately 5 minutes.

Baked Beans

Servings: 4

Cooking Time: 43 Minutes

Ingredients:

- 16 oz. pinto beans
- 8 cups water
- Salt to taste
- 8 slices bacon
- 1 onion, chopped
- 1/2 red bell pepper, chopped
- 2/3 cup barbecue sauce
- 1/2 cup ketchup
- 2 tablespoons mustard
- 1/4 cup cider vinegar
- 1 teaspoon liquid smoke
- 1/2 cup light brown sugar
- 1/2 cup water

Directions:

1. Add the beans, 8 cups of water, and salt in the Ninja Foodi. Cover the pot.
2. Set it to pressure.
3. Cook at high pressure for 25 minutes.
4. Release the pressure naturally.
5. Drain the beans and rinse with cold water.
6. Set the Ninja Foodi to sauté.
7. Add the bacon and cook until crispy.
8. Add the bell pepper and onion.
9. Cook for 3 minutes.
10. Add the rest of the ingredients.
11. Cover the pot. Set it to pressure.
12. Cook at high pressure for 15 minutes.
13. Release the pressure naturally.

Black-olive Burger With Japanese Vinegar Grilled

Servings: 5 Serves
Cooking Time: 25 Minutes

Ingredients:

- 4 slices of Swiss cheese.
- 2 tablespoons (30ml) of Chinese Chinkiang vinegar (kurozu)
- Kosher salt.
- 2 mayonnaise tablespoons (30ml)
- 2 tablespoons of black olives (about 15 pitted olives), chopped roughly.
- 12 ounces of freshly ground (340 g) beef, ideally 20% fat
- 2 brioche hamburger buns.

Directions:

1. In a medium bowl, mix beef gently and vinegar, only mix as long as it is necessary to combine them (overmixing the meat will make it to form a tighter and more meatloaf-like texture, so do not do it as necessary). Shape 2 patties slightly wider than the bun's width, press a dimple in the centre of each thumb and sauté with salt all over. Cool for a minimum of 30 minutes and up to 1 hour.

2. Meanwhile, whisk together olives and mayonnaise in a small bowl. Cool until ready to use.

3. Light one charcoal-filled chimney. When all the coal is lit and filled with grey ash, pour it out and disperse more than half the carbon grill equally. Alternatively, put half the gas grill burners in high heat. Set the grate in place, cover the grill, and allow 5 minutes of preheating. Wash the grilling grill and grease.

4. Place the patties directly over warm coals and cook, turning periodically on an instant-reading thermometer for about 7 minutes, until well charred and burgers centre register at 43 ° C (110 ° F). Continue to cook 2 slices of cheese until cheese is melted and burgers record 125 ° F for a medium-rare or 135 ° F (57 ° C) for a medium, 1 to 2 minutes longer. Move burgers to a large plate and leave for 5 minutes to rest. (Move burgers anytime to the cooler side of the grill if they start to fire, but are not yet in final internal temperature.)

5. Toast coals with buns. Spread the mayonnaise olive on top and bottom of each bowl. Place pads on lower buns, close burgers, and serve immediately.

Computer Tangerine Protein

Servings: 3 Serves
Cooking Time: 3 Minutes

Ingredients:

- 1 tangerine, peeled, quartered.
- 1/2 taste of ice.
- 2 almond scoops protein powder.
- 2 tiny ripe bananas, quarter sliced.
- 2 cups of coconut water chilled.
- 1 spinach cup.

Directions:

1. Put the high-speed blade in the jar and then add all ingredients in the order.
2. Pulse 3 times, then proceed for 60 seconds or until you reach the desired consistency.

Caramelized Mango Spears

Servings: 3
Cooking Time: 10 Mins

Ingredients:

- 1 cup of brown sugar
- 1 whole mango cut into spears
- ½ a cup of unsalted liquid butter
- ½ cup honey

Directions:

1. Place your Ninja Foodi grill grate in the unit and close the hood. Choose GRILL, set temperature to MAX, and set time to 10 minutes. Select START/STOP to start your pre-heating.
2. Whisk the ingredients except for the mango in a bowl, heating a little until runny
3. When the pre-heating timer goes off, place the mango on the grill and spread on the liquid mixture.
4. Close the hood and cook for five minutes
5. Flip the pineapple and apply the mixture to the other side, then close the hood and cook for another 5 minutes.
6. When the cooking is done, allow a little cooling before serving.

Scallops Au Gratin

Servings: Up To 4 People
Cooking Time: 15 - 30

Ingredients:

- scallops: 4
- breadcrumbs: 40 gr
- Parmesan cheese: 25 gr
- parsley spoon: 1
- olive oil: q.b.
- salt: q.b.
- garlic (optional): 1 clove

Directions:

1. Remove the mixer blade from the tank and insert the grid accessory.
2. Mix the breadcrumbs, parsley, cheese, garlic and salt in a bowl.
3. Place the scallops directly on top of the grill and cover them with the stuffing you prepared previously and sprinkle with a drizzle of oil.
4. Close the lid, select GRILL program, power level LOW, set 17min and press program start/stop key.
5. Before serving, spray with a drizzle of oil.

Pineapple Brazilian Grilled

Servings: 6 Serves
Cooking Time: 10 Minutes

Ingredients:

- 6 medium-sized wooden skewers (sweetened overnight in cold water)
- 3 slices of cocoon oil (melted)
- 35 g of cocoa sugar.
- 2 teaspoons nectar agave.
- 1 major ananas (peeled, cored).
- 1 teaspoon cinnamon ground.
- 1 lime juice.

Directions:

1. Start by cutting into 6 spears, your peeled and cored pineapple. Insert the wooden skewers in the base of each spear, which is the chunkiest, two-thirds of the way.
2. Put the grill in the unit and close the deck. Choose grill, set max, and time to ten minutes. To start, select start/stop.
3. While the unit is preheated, mix coconut oil, coconut sugar, agave nectar, and ground cinnamon into a shallow cup. Put in the mixture the pineapple spears and coat every spear evenly.
4. Once the device has preheated, place the spears carefully on the grill plate, close the cover, and cook 3 minutes before turning them with silicone tongs. Repeat throughout the cooking process until the grills on each side are well browned. It takes between 8 and 10 minutes.
5. Remove the grill, squeeze over the lime juice, and serve as soon as possible.

Burgers Smokey Black

Servings: 4 Serves
Cooking Time: 5 Minutes

Ingredients:

- 60 g gluten-free flat meal.
- 1 onion.
- 2 garlic cloves.
- 1/2 teaspoon flakes of chili.
- 1 gluten-free slice of bread.
- Fresh coriander 6 g
- 2 slices of olive oil.
- 1 egg (or vegan 'flaxseed egg' substituted)
- 2 teaspoons dried peppers.
- 1 teaspoon peppers.
- Tin black beans 1 x 400 g.
- 2 teaspoons ketchup tomatoes or puree tomatoes
- Salt & potato.

Directions:

1. Preheat the oven to 180 ° C
2. Drain the black beans and rinse thoroughly. Pat dry and spread over a baking tray evenly. Bake in the oven for about 5 minutes to dry a little.
3. Peel the onion and slice it finely. Add an olive oil saucepan and cook carefully until translucent. Make sure you also add the broken garlic cloves and sauté for another minute.
4. Fill your food processor with the slice of bread and pulse to produce breadcrumbs. In a bowl, put on one side.
5. Apply to your mixture and the pulsed black beans, onion, tomato ketchup, olive oil, candied paprika, paprika, chili flakes, coriander, salt, and pepper until the ingredients break down but not diluted.
6. Remove the meal and breadcrumbs. If the mix seems a bit wet, just add a little more flour.
7. Line a bakery with bakery paper.
8. Wet your hands a little (this helps the mixture), shape them into burger patties, and put them on the bakery. You should make four parts
9. Bake for about 15 minutes in the oven.
10. Serve immediately or hold in an airtight container in the fridge.

RECIPES INDEX

Printed in Poland
by Amazon Fulfillment
Poland Sp. z o.o., Wrocław
08 December 2021

2cd061ed-44f6-4bcb-96d7-ad53a8053692R01